Money Around the World

Spending Money

Rebecca Rissman

www.heinemann.co.uk/library

Visit our website to find out more information about Heinemann Library books.

To order:

 Phone 44 (0) 1865 888066

 Send a fax to 44 (0) 1865 314091

 Visit the Heinemann Bookshop at www.heinemann.co.uk/library to browse our catalogue and order online.

First published in Great Britain by Heinemann Library, Halley Court, Jordan Hill, Oxford OX2 8EJ, part of Harcourt Education. Heinemann is a registered trademark of Harcourt Education Ltd.

Editorial: Diyan Leake
Design: Joanna Hinton-Malivoire and Steve Mead
Picture research: Tracy Cummins and Heather Mauldin
Production: Duncan Gilbert

Origination: Chroma Graphics (Overseas) Pte Ltd
Printed and bound in China by South China Printing Company Ltd

ISBN 978 0 431 02526 1
12 11 10 09 08
10 9 8 7 6 5 4 3 2 1

British Library Cataloguing in Publicatin Data
Rissman, Rebecca
  Spending money. - (Money around the world)
  1. Consumption (Economics) - Juvenile literature
  I. Title
  339.4'7

Acknowledgments

The author and publisher are grateful to the following for permission to reproduce copyright material: © Alamy p. **10** (JL Images), **back cover** (JLImages); © Associated Press p. **11**; © Corbis pp. **4**, **6**, **17** (JAI/Michele Falzone), **23a** (Bob Krist), **23c** (Chuck Savage); © Getty Images pp. **5** (Oliver Benn), **7** (Chung Sug-Jun), **8** (AFP/Ramzi Haidar), **9** (Frederic J. Brown), **12**, **13** (Stewart Cohen), **14** (Andrew Hetherington), **16**, **20** (Celia Peterson), **21** (Chris Ryan), **23b** (Oliver Benn); © Istockphoto pp. **22a** (Ilya Genkin), **22b** (Sean Locke); © Jupiter Images p. **18** (Bananastock); © Shutterstock p. **22c** (Alexi Daniline); © The World Bank pp. **15** (Alan Gignoux), **19** (Tomas Sennett).

Cover photograph reproduced with permission of © Getty Images (AFP/Tengku Bahar).

Every effort has been made to contact copyright holders of any material reproduced in this book. Any omissions will be rectified in subsequent printings if notice is given to the publisher.

Contents

Spending money

People spend money to buy things.

People spend money in markets.

People spend money in shops.

People spend money in supermarkets.

Buying things

People spend money to buy different things.

People spend money on things
they want.

People spend money to buy food.

People spend money to buy cloth.

People spend money to buy clothes.

People spend money to buy toys.

Buying services

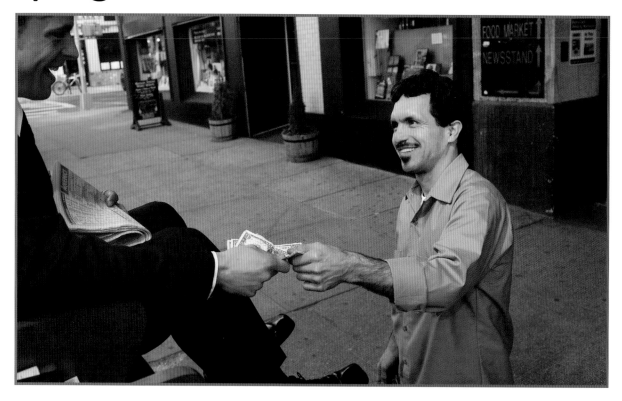

People spend money to buy services.

This means they pay people to do jobs for them.

People pay drivers to drive them.

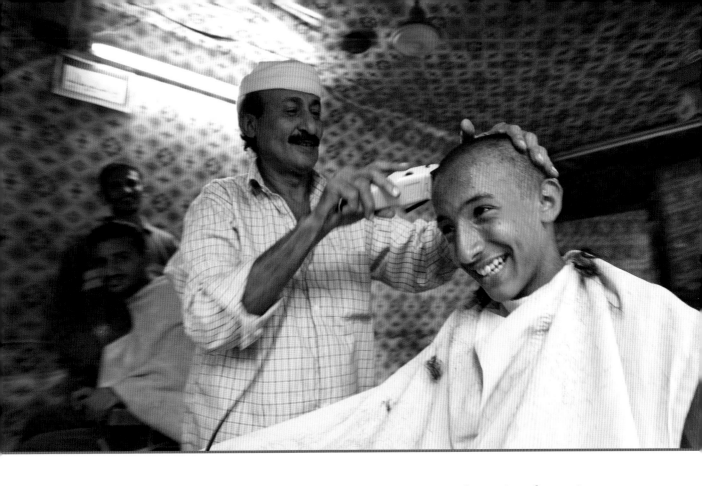

People pay barbers to cut their hair.

People pay babysitters to look after their children.

People pay builders to build houses.

Money around the world

All around the world, people
spend money.

But people also save money to
spend later.

Ways people spend money

People spend money with coins and notes.

People spend money with cheques.

People spend money with debit and credit cards.

Picture glossary

 **buy** pay for something with money

 **market** place where there are stalls with things to buy

 **shop** a building where there are things to buy. A shop is smaller than a supermarket.

Index

Notes for parents and teachers
Before reading
Ask the children why people have money. What things do they spend their money on? What do their parents have to buy with their money? Explain that money buys things but it is also used to pay for people to do things.
After reading
• Set up a role-play area as a supermarket. Encourage the children to price the different goods. Ask some children to be shop assistants, some to work at the check-out, and some to be customers.
• Make a chart with the heading: "People who help us". Ask the children to help you write a list of all the people who go to work to help other people, such as police, firefighters, doctors, and teachers.
• Sing the song: "Half a Pound of Tuppenny Rice".